W9-CJC-190

Cricut

for Beginners

A Practical Guide to Learn about the Different Types of Cricut Machines, Their Use and Understand Which Model Is Best Suited to Your Needs

MINERVA PETERS

© **Copyright 2021 by MINERVA PETERS - All rights reserved.**

This document is geared towards providing exact and reliable information in regards to the topic and issue covered. The publication is sold with the idea that the publisher is not required to render accounting, officially permitted, or otherwise, qualified services. If advice is necessary, legal or professional, a practiced individual in the profession should be ordered.

- From a Declaration of Principles which was accepted and approved equally by a Committee of the American Bar Association and a Committee of Publishers and Associations.

In no way is it legal to reproduce, duplicate, or transmit any part of this document in either electronic means or printed format. Recording of this publication is strictly prohibited, and any storage of this document is not allowed unless with written permission from the publisher. All rights reserved.

The information provided herein is stated to be truthful and consistent, in that any liability, in terms of inattention or otherwise, by any usage or abuse of any policies, processes, or Instructions contained within is the solitary and utter responsibility of the recipient reader. Under no circumstances will any legal responsibility or blame be held against the publisher for any reparation, damages, or monetary loss due to the information herein, either directly or indirectly.

Respective authors own all copyrights not held by the publisher.

The information herein is offered for informational purposes solely and is universal as such. The presentation of the information is without a contract or any type of guarantee assurance.

The trademarks used are without any consent, and the publication of the trademark is without permission or backing by the trademark owner. This book's trademarks and brands are for clarifying purposes only owned by the owners, not affiliated with this document.

Table of Contents

Introduction

Cricut is the name of the brand for a machine that cuts a paper, vinyl, card, and if you have the professional model, fabrics. It deals through an online program called Design Space, which allows you to purchase, upload, or develop designs, which the Cricut would then cut for you. It also has a print and cut function that helps you print a pattern on a standard home printer and then cut it to size with the Cricut machine. You can buy extra tools for your Cricut that will let you write in fancy calligraphy, perforate sections or score, and emboss or engrave intricate designs in addition to cutting.

There are older & newer versions and standard, premium, and more complex options, much like for many other digital devices.

In terms of success and home crafting, Silhouette is the most likely competitor of the Cricut machine. Silhouette machines are somewhat similar to Cricut machines in terms of functionality; for example, Silhouette Studio is the Silhouette's equivalent of Design Space. Silhouette machines, including Cricut machines, come in a variety of models. The key Silhouette options are mentioned below, along with some of their advantages and disadvantages.

Cricut devices are die-cutting devices (also known as cutting plotters) that can cut a wide range of materials based on the model. Paper, vinyl, cardstock, packaging, and several other items may be cut with the Cricut Explore Air. Many different varieties of fabric, thin wood, and leather are available with the Cricut Maker. Cricut machines may also be used to build scoring lines as well as draw pictures and text. On Cricut's website, you'll find a comprehensive list of what each computer will cut.

Since these devices may deal with quite a diverse variety of products, there are a variety of applications. Cricut machines are common with crafters for making greeting cards, scrapbooking, paper crafts, and iron-on designs for T-shirts. Another common use for Cricut vinyl decals is making personalized mugs and tumblers. The list continues on and on for party decorations, wall paintings, personalized posters, and stickers.

Cricut Explore Air is the most sophisticated electronic cutting device for DIY fans, allowing you to go from inspiration to development. For wireless cutting, this device includes Bluetooth technology. With the latest Cricut Design Space iPad software, you can use your phone, notebook, or iPad.

Chapter 1. What Is Cricut?

A Cricut is an electric cutting machine that can cut various materials such as paper, vinyl, cardboard, and iron-on transfers into various designs. Both leather and wood can be cut with certain Cricut machines!

The Cricut will cut almost everything that will otherwise be cut using scissors and also an X-acto knife. However, a Cricut machine can cut with much greater accuracy and speed than can be achieved by hand!

If you're an experienced DIYer or a beginner, Cricut® can make it simple to create custom, professional-quality projects. You can cut and make interior decoration designs, parties and celebrations, marriages, clothing, and more with our smart cutting machines.

Cricut machines are equipped with a comprehensive online manual and a variety of other Cricut tools, making them relatively simple to learn how to operate. Both Work Space and the Cricut machine are built to be simple to use, and you don't need a lot of graphic design skills to use them. There's a library of photos and designs in the Cricut Design space that you can easily import as just a new project. Some are unrestricted, while others may be bought for a small fee.

1.1 What Can You Make With A Cricut Machine?

A Cricut is indeed a home cutting machine that can be used for a variety of projects.

Vinyl, parchment, poster board, cardboard, foam board, felt, cloth, leather, and dozens of other items may be cut with Cricut machines. This is the place to be.

If you've got a Cricut Maker cutting unit, you can use the knife blade to cut balsa wood and other tougher materials and the rotary cutter to cut other fabrics and crepe paper.

You can also do carvings, perforating, wany lines, even debossing with the modern Cricut Maker tools.

You will use a Cricut cutting machine to make stuff like:

- Custom T-Shirts

- Paper Flowers

- Earrings + other Jewelry

- Banners

- Stencils

- Stickers

- Key chains

- Wood Cutouts

- Decals

- And more a lot

1.2 How Cricut Machines Work?

A Cricut cutting system may be compared to a home printer. Instead of printing the design onto a sheet, a Cricut machine cuts the design from a sheet of paper using a thin, movable blade (or other material.)

To start, use Cricut design software or app to build a design. Then, using Bluetooth or USB, you send the project to the Cricut cutting unit. The template is fed into the Cricut system, which then cuts it out with a small, precise blade.

You may use a wireless connection to link a Cricut to your device, make or save designs on your computer, and then send it to your Cricut to cut. Design Space (windows,

Mobile, and mobile phone) is Cricut's app that helps you build and import templates to cut using your machine. A small blade (or rotary cutter, or scoring tool, or pen) is housed within the Cricut. After you've created a design in Design Space, you may place your preferred material on a 12-inch broad cutting mat, wirelessly transfer your design to your Cricut, and then put your material into the machine. Your project will start cutting as soon as you press a key.

Here's about using a Cricut in basic words.

- Begin by placing your cutting material on the adhesive cutting mat. (While the Cricut allows the cuts, the cutting pad keeps the material in place.) Place the mat in the unit and turn it on.

- Next, open Cricut Design Space and choose a design. Send the pattern to your Cricut machine after selecting your content settings.

- To begin cutting, push a button on your Cricut device.

- Detach the mat from the machine and the content from the mat until the machine has finished cutting.

1.3 Three Types Of Cricut Machines For Beginners

In the latest Cricut lineup, there are three separate cutting machines. All had advantages and disadvantages.

Cricut Explore

Cricut's best-selling machine is the Explore Air 2. It's a wonderful mid-level model that's suitable for both beginners and advanced crafters.

It may cut over a hundred different fabrics, including paper, vinyl, cardstock, certain forms of cloth, and stabilized clothing.

The Cricut Explore will create full-size iron-on stickers for T-shirts, big vinyl decals, and 3D paper projects using mats 12 x 12 inches to 12 x 24 inches.

Cricut Maker

Cricut Maker is the company's most efficient and costly cutting machine. It's a significant improvement over the Explore unit.

The Cricut Maker is a cutting machine that is both durable and flexible. It will cut over 300 different products, including wood, cloth, felt, silk, acrylic, and plastic, among several others. It may also be used for mats measuring 12 x 12 inches or 12 x 24 inches.

It's capable of more than just cutting and pasting. The knife blade, engraving edge, foiling tip, debossing method, and rotary cutter are compatible with the Cricut maker's ever-expanding range of blades and accessories.

Cricut Joy

The Cricut Joy is now the latest edition from Cricut. It's a handy little machine that's simple to set up and to use. Paper, plastic, iron-on, and certain thin fake leathers are among the fabrics it can cut.

Since this device has a smaller footprint, it's simple to store in a little craft space. It is, in my experience, the only Cricut machine that is completely "portable."

A pattern with a full width of 5.5" can be sliced with the Cricut Joy. As a result, it's ideal for creating stamps, signs, greeting cards, and other tiny crafts. Although it isn't as versatile as the bigger machines, it is still a fantastic machine for studying the basics.

1.4 Which Is The Best Cricut Machine For A Beginner?

The Cricut Explore Air 2 is the perfect Cricut machine for a beginner on a budget. Cricut's most famous machine is the Cricut Explore Air 2, and with good purpose! It will cut over 100 different materials, from cardstock, plastic, iron-on, or

specialty papers, cork, and bonded leather. It isn't the quickest and quietest cutting machine on the market, but it gets the job done and is user-friendly.

Chapter 2. Cricut Machines Models

Do you want to buy a Cricut machine but aren't sure which one to get? Maybe you're thinking of buying one of the older versions secondhand, but you're hesitant because you don't know much about them...? You've come to the right spot.

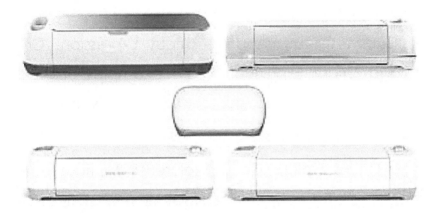

Let us start at the beginning. Provo Craft created all of the Cricut machines mentioned below. The first Cricut machines only operated with cartridges, but Provo Craft wasn't left behind for long and produced some fantastic goods thanks to technical advancements. Some names are mentioned in sequential order because some crafters are still interested in older versions, mostly since they do not require computers to operate.

2.1 Latest Cricut Machines

There are currently three Cricut cutting machines available.

- Cricut Joy

- Cricut Maker

- And the Cricut Explore Air 2

Cricut Gypsy, Cricut Personal, Cricut Expression, Cricut Cake, and Cricut Expression 2 are examples of legacy devices that are no longer sold. Cricut is no longer supporting these units.

The initial Cricut Explore, Cricut Explore Air & Cricut Explore One have all recently been discontinued. Cricut also supports these three Explore machines, and they function with the newest release of Cricut Design Space.

Cricut Joy

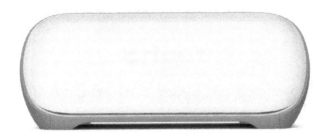

Cricut Joy is a little cutting machine around half the size of the Cricut Explore & Cricut Maker. It's a little simpler than the other Cricut devices, with just one blade and a pen holder. The diameter of the cut is 4.5 inches.

But don't be fooled by its diminutive size—it has some exciting new features! Mat-free cutting, which allows you to cut up to 20 feet (yes, 20 feet) for "Smart vinyl" in one go, is one of them. Cricut Joy also comes with a Card Mat, which makes creating cards for all purposes.

Cricut Maker

Cricut Maker is the company's most advanced cutting machine. It has a similar appearance to the Explore series of machines, but it's been completely redesigned from scratch. It does all that the Cricut Explore does, along with a few extras.

The tiny Rotary Blade on the Cricut Maker cuts unboned cloth (so you wouldn't need a stabilizer as you do with all the Cricut Explore line). This machine even cuts felt wonderful, so if you want to make felt crafts, this is the machine for you.

The Knife Blade on the Cricut Maker will cut thicker materials (upto 3/32"), including balsa wood & thick leather. The Scoring Wheel will score a variety of materials.

Four innovative resources were revealed in July 2019. Here we will show you how to use both of these tools:

- The Debossing Tool

- The Engraving Tool

- The Perforation Tool

- The Wavy Rotary Tool

Cricut Maker's adaptive tool system was designed to be expandable, which means it can be used with equipment that Cricut hasn't even dreamed about yet! They're testing a dozen more software, but this machine will be able to do even more as the latest tools are launched.

The price range is the highest throughout the Cricut line— $399, with a sale of $349 on sometimes. This device is for you whether you're a professional crafter who wants to deal with a range of fabrics, or if you're a sewing lover, an avid paper crafter, or even a woodworker.

12x12 to 12x24 mat scale (inches)

True Image Cut Height is 0.25 to 11.5" tall & 11.5" or 23.5" long (depending on mat size).

It has a "print then cut" function that helps you to cut out a picture that has already been written.

It is cutting hundreds of different fabrics for the Adaptive Tool System. It differs from previous machines in that it has a modern fabric rotary blade and a knife blade for tougher materials.

This machine is the most recent to enter the market. The blade's level of pressure while cutting is much higher, allowing the creator to cut much heavier materials like leather or thicker material.

Provo Craft is continuously upgrading the design lab, and they're likely working on a new machine right now.

Cricut Explore Air 2

This machine is a true workhorse, capable of cutting plastic, iron-on, cardstock, fake leather, Cricut felt, and over 100 other materials. While it cannot cut the heavier materials that the Maker would, it is a wonderful machine for most crafters. It even comes in a variety of colors to complement every craft room!

12x12 & 12x24 mat scale (inches)

True Image Cut Height is 0.25 to 11.5" tall & 11.5" or 23.5" long (depending on mat size).

It has a "print then cut" function that helps you to cut out a picture that has already been written.

There are two instrument holders, one for a pen and the other for the blade. It's even possible to do it with a deep-cut blade.

To put it another way, Air 2 is quite similar to Air 1. The cutting pace is the only distinction.

Around the same period, Provo Craft launched a new range of items, with the subsequent devices being able to cut tougher materials. The prospective buyer demand has swelled dramatically due to the addition of fiber to one of the fabrics.

Cricut Explore Air

Cricut no longer sells this machine, but it can still be found. The Cricut Explore Air moves down from the Circut Air 2, but it has two features: the Cricut Explore one doesn't really: it is Bluetooth-enabled. Therefore, you wouldn't have to plug it in and has a secondary tool holder to write, score, and cut all at once.

True Image Cut Height is 0.25 to 11.5" tall & 11.5" or 23.5" long (depending on mat size).

It has a "print then cut" function that helps you to cut out a picture that has already been written.

There are two instrument holders, one for a pen and the other for the blade. It's even possible to do it with a deep-cut blade.

Explore Air isn't something that dissimilar to Explore. The main distinction is that Air is wireless, while the older Explore attaches to your device with a cord. It has already been reported that the Explore machine has a wireless adapter, so you don't need to upgrade to Explore Air 1 to get wireless capabilities.

Cricut Explore One

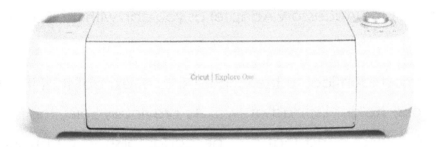

This machine isn't any longer accessible from Cricut, but it is still available secondhand. Cricut Explore One is most simple and cost-effective unit currently available from Cricut. It has all of the Explore Air machines' accurate cutting, printing, and scoring skills, and it can cut all of the same materials (over 100!). It isn't Bluetooth-enabled (which means you'll have to connect it to your device with a cable), and it doesn't have a dual tool cartridge, so you can't compose and cut in same pass.

12x12 & 12x24 mat scale in inches

True Image Cut Scale is 0.25-11.5 inches tall by 11.5" or 23.5 inches long (depending on mat size).

There's a "print then cut" option that lets you cut out a picture that's already been written.

There is just one blade or pen holder, but that does not restrict you. You will get the same performance with the Explore One Accessory Adapter as you can with the Explore unit.

It's almost identical to the Cricut Explore, except that it just has one holder instead of two. As previously said, this is a simple workaround that can be accomplished by buying an adapter.

2.2 Old Cricut Cutting Machines

There are different models of Cricut machines which Circuit no more supports, here are their names and specification for a quick look to know about;

Personal (Original) Cricut Machine

- True Image Cut Size: 1" - 5.5" tall and up to 11.5" long

- The gadget does not need a device to operate. It works for cartridges that must be placed through a slot to cut out pictures

- Please notice that Cricut cartridges are being phased out in favor of digital files, and they could be phased out entirely shortly.

- The blade is moved using a four-way button on the machine.

- Cricut Gypsy is compatible with this machine.

- Cricut Craft Space is compatible with this unit.

Cricut Create

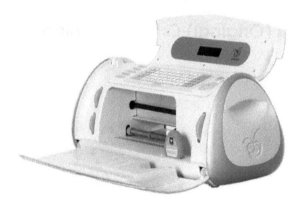

- Mat size 6x12 inch

- Image Cut Size is 0.25 to 5,5" tall & 11.5" long

- • The unit would not need the use of a device to function. It works for cartridges that must be placed through a slot to cut out pictures. Please be aware that Cricut cartridges are being phased out in favor of digital files, and they could be phased out entirely shortly.

- The machine has an 8-direction blade movement

button

- The machine is Cricut Gypsy compliant

- Cricut Craft Space is compatible with this unit Portrait button for taller images

- Fit page mode available

- Flip image function

- Center Point Function

- Autofill mode

Expression 1

- Mat size 12x12 and 12x24 inch

- Image Cut Size is 0.25 to 11.5" tall & 11.5" or (depending on mat size) 23.5" long

- The unit would not need the use of a device to function. It works for cartridges that must be placed through a slot to cut out pictures. Please notice that Cricut cartridges are being phased out in favor of digital files, and they could be phased out entirely shortly. The machine has an eight directional button for moving the blade

- Compatible with Cricut Craft Room

- Compatible with Cricut Gypsy

- Portrait key for taller images

- Fit length mode

- Fit page mode available

- Autofill mode

- Flip image function

- Center Point Function

- Line Return function

Expression 2

- The original purchase price was 149 dollars (No longer sold)

- True Image Cut Scale is 0.25 to 11.5" tall & 11.5" or (depending on mat size) 23.5" long

- Mat size (inch) 12x12 or 12x24

- The unit would not need the use of a device to function. It works for cartridges that must be placed through a slot to cut out pictures. Please notice that Cricut cartridges are being phased out in favor of digital files, and they could be phased out entirely shortly.

- Cricut Gypsy is compatible with this unit.

- is Cricut Craft Room compliant

- Match to the page, fit to length, autofill, center point, flip picture, line return, quantity choices, paper saver, and shadow alternative are all available on this machine.

- The improved pace and pressure controls

- Rotation of the image

Imagine

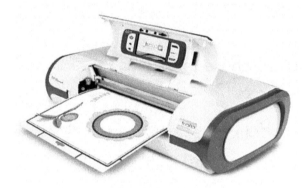

- True Image Cut Height is 0.25- 11.5" tall by 11.5" or (depending on mat size) 23.5" long

- The unit does not need the use of a monitor to operate. It works for cartridges that must be placed through a slot to cut out pictures. Please notice that Cricut cartridges are being phased out in favor of digital files, and they could be phased out entirely shortly.

- Cricut Gypsy is compatible with this unit.

- Cricut Craft Room is compatible with this unit

- Match to the page, fit to length, autofill, center point, flip picture, line return, quantity choices, paper saver, shadow choice, colored LCD screen, and image rotation option is included in the machine.

- It prints and cuts using HP ink cartridges 97 (tricolor) and 98 (black) (98 black)

- This is the only older unit that will use Cricut Imagine cartridges.

Cricut Mini

- True Image Cut Height is 0.25- 11.5" tall by 11.5" or

(depending on mat size) 23.5" broad

- The unit was designed exclusively to be used with computers and utilizes the Cricut craft room program as its operating software.

- Cricut Gypsy is compatible with this unit.

Cricut Explore

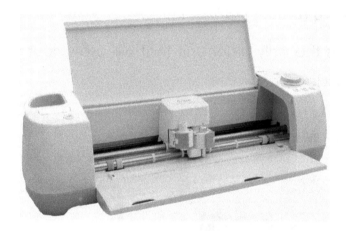

- True Picture Cut Size is 0.25 to 11.5" tall & 11.5" or (depending on mat size) 23.5" long

- It has a "print then cut" option that helps you to cut out an image that has already been printed.

- It has a dual tool holder, one for the pen and the other for the blade. It's even possible to do it with a deep-cut blade.

- You can purchase a wireless adapter to link your Explore to your computer instead of using a cord.

Chapter 3. How To Use Cricut Machines?

Cricut machines are equipped with a complete online manual and various other Cricut tools, making them relatively simple to learn how to operate. Both Design Space & the Cricut machine are built to be easy to use, and you don't need a lot of graphic design skills to use them (it does help if you need to create your projects from scratch). There's a library of photos and designs in Cricut Design space that you can easily import as a fresh project. Some are unrestricted, while others may be bought for a little fee.

3.1 A Beginner's Guide To Using A Cricut Machine

If there is one question we get asked every week, it is generally about **operating** a Cricut machine.

The Cricut Explore Air 2 & Cricut Maker.

One of our favorite things about these fabric cutting machines is how easy they are to use — but they can take some getting used to, particularly if you're new to craft cutting.

With that in mind, we've put together a comprehensive beginner's guide to **using Cricut** Explore Air 2 & Cricut Maker.

We'll get straight to the point, breaking down and process into its most simple components so you can get what you're searching for as quickly and efficiently as possible.

In no time, you'll be cutting like a professional!

First and foremost, let's examine the machine itself and determine what each function does.

Cricut Explore Air 2

1. Button to open the Main lid

2. Dial Smart Set

3. Power on/off

4. The Dual carriage (where the blades & pens are housed when working)

5. Accessory cup

6. Accessory drawers

7. Cartridge port (which you can plug any cartridges)

Cricut Maker

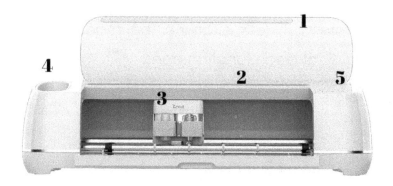

As you can see, it is a little sleeker & less cluttered as compared to the Explore Air 2.

1. Soft open main lid

2. Tablet/phone holder with a port for charging

3. Dual tool carriage

4. Tool cups with Rubber Bottom

5. Control panel

3.2 Space Creating for the Cricut

You'll need to set up your new Cricut machine now that it's unpacked and ready to use.

All you need now is a flat surface with an electricity connection; if you have a designated craft space or are merely crafting on the dining room table — note, you can still use an extension lead unless you can't get near enough to a plug!

Make sure there's enough room around the Cricut for you to conveniently load mats into and out of the unit.

If it's in place, connect the machine into a wall socket (a power cord is supplied with every purchase), then click the 'open' button on the Explore Air 2's lid (feature #1 in the diagram above) or softly open the Maker's lid to get your newish machine up and running.

You'll now need to set up the computer you'll be designing nearby. A full desktop system, a notebook, a smartphone, or even your phone may be included.

Ensure that you have internet connections to download and use the Cricut Design Space software (more on that later). You can now build and cut without being linked to the internet, but the initial download would need a connection.

One of both devices' best features is that they are wireless, meaning you don't have to connect your device to the machine until you can start designing.

You'll be able to wirelessly link your device and Cricut once you've signed into the Design Space app.

3.3 How to Use Design Space?

A piece of paper guiding you to install Cricut Design Space will be included in the box with your new craft cutting machine.

If you can't find it, go to cricut.com/setup on the computer, desktop, smartphone, or phone that you'll be using to make designs for your Cricut.

This guide will take you through the setup phase step by step, plugin and switch on your machine if you haven't done so already.

To begin, ensure that Bluetooth is turned on your computer, tablet, or phone.

Depending on the model, the Bluetooth option is usually

included in the 'Settings' section — only make sure it's turned on.

Switch on your Cricut if you haven't already by momentarily keeping down the power key on the right side of the unit (#3 in the diagram above and on the Maker's control panel). Look for your gadget in the gadgets list when you open the Bluetooth settings on your phone or tablet. When you come across it, press on it and select Link.

You may be asked to enter a password at this point; if so, enter 0000.

If you can't get the Bluetooth to function for some purpose or don't have it on your laptop, attach your machine and the Cricut with the supplied USB cable instead.

When you're done, your device and Cricut will be connected and ready to use.

Now it's only a matter of being creative!

What's awesome regarding Design Space is it's built specifically for beginners, so it gives you step-by-step instructions on how to begin and complete each project. It's so easy to be using that more advanced users can find it restricting — but that's something you should think about later!

3.4 Using the Design Space App

Since the software is cloud-based, you'll be able to view your designs and account from every smartphone that has the app installed.

It's perfect for people who fly or need connections to their Cricut account while they don't have access to the internet.

To build offline, simply ensure that you have downloaded all of the icons and fonts you'll need ahead of time. Click the save button, pick 'save as,' and export to your desktop to save **offline use tasks**. Simply pull down the options menu and click 'My Projects on this iPad' (or whatever gadget you're using), and launch it from there when you want to reach your projects when you're offline.

When you're at online **M**ode, you'll be able to see the hundreds of various projects available in the app, as well as the option to build designs from scratch using the 'fresh canvas' tool.

3.5 Your First Cut

Most new Cricut users can begin their cutting journey by completing the "Enjoy Card" project that comes with the machine when it is purchased.

It is an excellent opportunity to ease into the art cutting field and get acquainted with the various ways of using the Cricut Machine.

Design Space will notify you to begin this project after you've connected your machine and Cricut.

Everything you have to do is obey the onscreen step-by-step directions and use the equipment and accessories that came with the kit.

Once you've finished the first cut, you'll probably feel more secure in taking on more exciting and challenging tasks.

3.6 Using the Cricut Explore Air 2

Now it's time to learn how to use some of the Cricut Explore Air 2's exclusive features.

The Smart Set Dial, located on the machine's right side, is a tool that will make your life simpler.

It's just a material collection dial that's pre-programmed with the appropriate settings for whatever material you're working with that day.

If you're cutting a sticker, for example, you'll click 'Cardstock' on the dial. The machine would then choose the appropriate blade settings for you, such as depth, rpm, and force, so you don't have to.

The most often used materials have been cleverly included on the dial by Cricut:

- Paper

- Iron-On

- Vinyl

- Light Cardstock

- Cardstock

- Poster Board

- Fabric

On the dial, you'll also see half settings between the substances. This is about when you need a little less, or a few more pressure than the preset settings would provide.

If you're cutting light cardstock and the blade isn't cutting the design fully, use the half setting among Light & Cardstock. Alternatively, if you're cutting the poster board as well as the blade is putting too much weight on the mat by cutting it away, change the configuration to Fabric & Poster Board.

You can then choose the exact material you're working with from Design Space's extensive drop-down menu, and

the Cricut can change its blade settings for you, so you don't have to.

Fast Mode

Fast Mode is another fantastic aspect of the Cricut Explore Air 2.

In Fast Mode, your Explore Air 2 will compose and cut up to twice as quickly as normal — that's a significant time saver!

However, it isn't usable for every material and is best seen for simplified projects.

Fast Mode can be used for the following materials:

- Iron

- Vinyl

- Cardstock

- Light Cardstock

To activate Fast Mode, press Set, Load, Go screen & check the box next to the Dial Position indicator.

Simply click the Pause key under the Smart Set Dial & switch it off in Design Space if you begin cutting and forget to activate Fast Mode — or if you want to interrupt it.

One thing to keep in mind is that the machine is very noisy in Fast Mode; if you reside with anyone, it's possibly better to stop using it late at night!

Chapter 4. Maintenance Of The Cricut Machines

The Cricut cutting machine is an incredible piece of technology. It allows us to make a variety of wonderful things. However, the cuts aren't quite as tidy as we'd like, and it's not always clear why or how to fix it. So, those are the five items to keep in mind while cutting with your Cricut Explore or any Cricut machine. You can use this to fix almost every Cricut cutting issue and make those perfect, clean cuts!

4.1 Routine Maintenance Of Your Cricut Machines

As with anything else in life, if you take care of it, it would last longer. Sometimes people need care.

Cleaning the Cricut Machines

- With a damp cloth, gently wipe exterior panels.

- Immediately dry excess moisture with a soft cloth.

- Do not scrub the unit with additives or alcohol-based cleaners (such as acetone, benzene, or carbon tetrachloride). Cleansers and washing machines that scratch the skin can also be avoided. Please do not submerge the unit or any of its components in water.

- Make Sure to keep away from food & liquids; try not to consume or drink when using the machine; and store in a safe, dust-free setting.

- Avoid extremes of heat and cold, and don't keep the unit in the vehicle, where the heat might melt or destroy the plastic parts.

- Should not subject yourself to intense sunshine for long periods of time.

- You can get spare parts for Cricut machines directly from Cricut.

4.2 Grease Application Instructions

- Disconnect the Cricut Explore computer from the power source.

- Shift the Cut Smart carriage to the left by gently moving it.

- Wipe the Cut Smart carriage bar clean with a tissue all the way through.

- Move that Cut Smart carriage to the right by gently moving it.

- Wipe around the whole Cut Smart carriage bars with a

tissue and repeat the cleaning procedure.

- Slowly move the carriage to the machine's middle.

- Squeeze a little volume of grease onto the ends of the cotton swab after opening the lubricant box.

- Spread a thin layer of grease around the bar on all sides of its Smart carriage to build a 1/4-inch rim on either edge.

- To evenly spread the grease across the whole bar, slowly move the Smart carriage to the left & then back to the centre.

- Wipe some oil buildup off the ends of the bar.

4.3 How To Get The Cleanest Cuts?

Your MAT, MATERIAL, BLADE, SETTING, and PATTERN are the five aspects to pay attention to.

4.4 Use A Sticky Mat

To get clean cuts, your Cricut mat should be quite sticky. So, if your cuts aren't neat, the first thing you can do is change mats. It typically turns to a newer or finer mat, which immediately fixes the problem. If you can't afford a fresh pad, you can make your current one stickier by cleaning it with dishwashing soap and letting it air dry.

4.5 Use Always A Clean, Sharp Blade

Please make sure the Cricut blade is clean & sharp before using it. You can do this by rolling up a sheet of aluminum foil in this manner. Then take the blade out of its casing, depress the plunger, then carefully put it into and out of the aluminum ball — maybe 50 times. This appears to sharpen the blade while simultaneously cleaning some residue off it, such as pieces of paper or vinyl that might stick to it. (It may or may not be sharpening it. However, it does the work!) The Fine-Point & Deep-Point Blades will also be used for this technique.

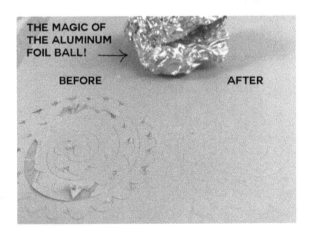

You may be using the wrong blade if the issue isn't that the blade isn't cutting all the way, though, but rather that it's cutting So Far. Check the packaging; the Cricut Explore & Cricut Maker needs the Premium Fine-Point blade (German Carbide). The caps' color on the Premium Fine-Point Blades could be distinguished from their packaging, which is either WHITE or RED. The grey cap blades are not compatible with the Cricut Explores & Makers because they were designed for older Cricut machines; also, they are too big.

4.6 Use Quality Materials

It's also possible that the kind of substance you use has an impact on how well it cuts. Not every document, for example, is made equal. You'll get more tearing if the paper's fibers are lighter or shorter, as is common with lower-quality paper. If the paper really doesn't seem to be cutting properly despite using a good sticky mat and a new blade, it's possible that the paper is to blame. There have been several times.

4.7 Check Pattern

Not all patterns will cut perfectly. The smaller, more complex, and complicated they are, the more difficult they are to cut. They are often simply too small. That might be an alternative, and you should try having them larger. If that doesn't fit or isn't a choice, consider setting the content to Intricate Cuts if you are cutting cardstock. When you're cutting vinyl, try the setting of washi tape. While none of these methods is sure to succeed, it's worth the try. Finally, certain patterns can be too small or complex to be cut without problems. This doesn't mean anything is lost; you may be able to cut it and clean it up later with scissors or a knife.

Chapter 5. Tool And Accessories

It's easy to get confused when you get your Cricut and see how much to explore. There are a variety of gadgets and equipment to choose from! How do you decide whether to purchase? How can you figure out which techniques would be more beneficial to you and you're crafting?

Do you have a new Cricut and aren't sure what accessories you'll need to get started? The essential Cricut accessories & supplies you'll need to get started creating amazing stuff right away!

Cricut Tools & Accessories, That Use In Crafting

5.1 Weeder

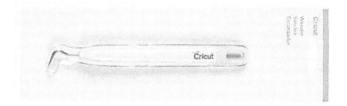

Whenever it comes to Cricut crafting, this tool is a must-have! If you haven't heard about weeding before, you will shortly. When you use your Cricut to cut materials like vinyl and iron-on, you'll need to scrape the excess material from outside and within the design. You're essentially taking away the white space so you can focus on the plan. You'll need a weeder at some point in your life, believe me. This Weeder Tool Kit is one of the favorites since it has some different weeders. To be frank, must buy weeder equipment at a discount because of a poor habit of misplacing them.

5.2 Scraper

5.3 Basic Tool Set

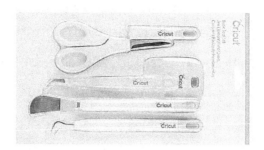

One of our most common toolsets is this five-piece kit. It includes five items, two of which we've already discussed: a weeder and a scraper, as well as scissors, tweezers & spatula. If you're just getting started with Cricut, this is a fantastic toolset to get! We've already discussed how fantastic the weeder & scraper are. Now let's move on to the other three tools.

5.4 Scoring Stylus

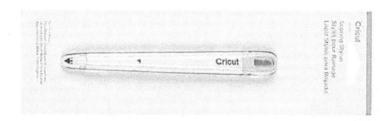

If you like making paper crafts, the scoring stylus is an

excellent method to have on hand. Your Cricut will hold the scoring stylus to build fold lines for you. You can now create cards, boxes, envelopes, 3D projects, and more with ease! The Cricut Explore Air 2 & the Cricut Maker both will use the scoring stylus. For Maker mates, you can even use the Scoring Wheel, which works almost as well.

5.5 Paper Tool Set

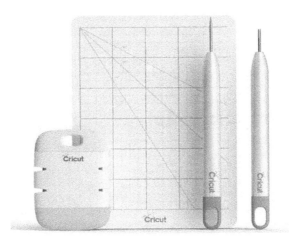

5.6 Sewing Kit

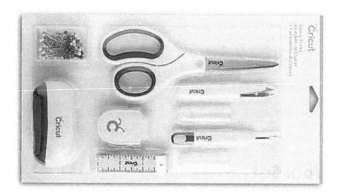

5.7 Self-Healing Rotary Mat

5.8 TrueControl Knife

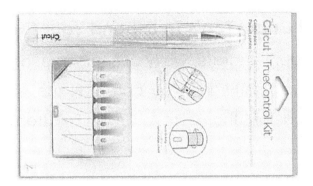

The TrueControl Knife is the last but not least. This knife is similar to a Xacto knife, except it's even stronger! As compared to a Xacto knife, the TrueControl Knife has

greater control over the tasks due to its design. It can cut a range of materials, including paper, cardstock, thin plastics, cloth, and fabric. It has a rubber handle that makes it easy to hold, and it arrives with five replacement blades so you can swap it out without touching the metal.

Chapter 6. Cricut Maker Tools

6.1 A List of Cricut Tools To Expand Your Creativity

You can grade, perforate, wavy cut, engrave, and deboss with QuickSwap software. You can now use your Cricut Maker to add foil, thanks to   Cricut Foil Transfer Tool's invention!

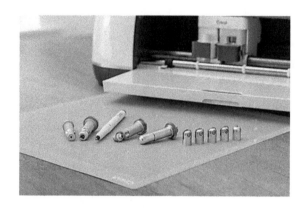

Wavy Blade, Debossing Tip, Perforation Blade, & Engraving Tip.

Find out all about each of these great tools in the sections below.

6.2 What Makes Cricut Maker Different From Cricut's Other Machines?

Many of you might also be wondering what sets Cricut Maker apart from the Cricut Explore group of machines if you're considering issues like.

What will Cricut Explore machine can't do, and what can other machines do.?

Is it worthwhile to upgrade from a Cricut Explore to a Cricut Maker?

What exactly is Design Space, and how does it vary depending on the machine?

We've seen you, and we want to be sure you've had answers to as many of your concerns as possible. So, how would the Cricut Maker compare favorably against the Cricut Explore family of machines? The Cricut Explore Air, Cricut Explore Air 2, Cricut Explore One, and Cricut Explore are all included.

6.3 More Possibilities With More Tools

Let's begin with the Cricut Maker's Adaptive Tool System, which is the most significant difference between the two machines. The Adaptive Tool System, which helps us extend the suite of software you will use for various cutting and scoring applications, is a brand-new technology integrated into the Cricut Maker.

The Adaptive Tool System will shift the tools up and down, lift and turn, and cut from side to side, allowing you to cut more products with even more pressure than ever. It allows the all-new Rotary Blade to cut through fabrics without a backer (straight off the bolt). Below, we'll go through the Rotary Blade in more detail. Cricut Maker may cut a wide range of products, including delicate papers and fabrics and denser materials such as leather, chipboard, balsa wood, and more.

6.4 Cricut Maker With 10X The Cutting Power

Our Cricut Explore machines feature a drag blade technology mechanism that goes up, down, and side-to-side when cutting. Although a variety of fantastic materials can also be cut, they must be stabilized, or the blade might get stuck in the fiber. Since the Cricut Explore Family lacks the same strain as the Cricut Maker, it's often challenging to cut through thick materials like basswood, balsa wood, and leather. We would like you to know what tools you should use for which machine now that we've clarified the technology gaps between the Cricut machine lines.

Fine Point Blades, Rotary Blades, Single Scoring Wheels, and Knife Blades are available from Cricut.

The Cricut Maker works using all of the same materials as you use with the Cricut Explore group of machines. Deep Point Blades, Fine Point Blades, Bonded Fabric Blades, Scoring Stylus, & Cricut Pens are all included.

The Knife Blade, Rotary Blade, Single & Double Scoring Wheels, Perforation Blade, Wavy Blade, Fine Debossing Tip & Engraving Tip are among the latest tools developed especially for Cricut Maker thanks to the Adaptive Tool System.

Rotary Blade

For the first time, Rotary Blade introduces endlessly customizable, precise fabric cutting to the house. It can be used to cut fleece, cotton, denim, and other materials. It cuts almost every fabric easily and reliably – without the use of backing material – thanks to its gliding, rolling movement. The Cricut Maker comes with a Rotary Blade.

Knife Blade (Extra Deep)

The extra-deep Knife Blade, which is much like an automatic X-ACTO® blade, cuts through dense materials about 2.4 mm (3/32") thick with remarkable ease and safety. It works well for heavier materials such as balsa wood, matboard, or hard leather. More information on the Knife Blade can be found here.

Scoring Wheels (single and double) create a deep single-line score that's ideal for uncoated light materials include light cardstock, crepe paper, and even acetate.

The Double Scoring Wheel produces two deep, parallel score lines on coated, heavier materials like cardboard and poster board.

Wavy Blade

The Wavy Blade gives every style a whimsical wavy edge in half the time of a drag blade. It's especially chiseled stainless steel blade is ideal for creating original decals, envelopes, invitations, gift tags & college projects, as well as any other project that needs beautifully polished edges and trendy style accents. Learn about the various materials that the Wavy Blade might cut.

Perforation Blade

With specific perforation cuts on a lot of projects, you can get the ideal tear quickly and easily. Perforation lines that are evenly spaced allow for smooth, even tearing and no need to fold – particularly useful for curved shapes! We love these Perforation Blade projects in Design Space because they produce unique punches outs that allow you to engage with your design long after it's finished!

Fine Debossing Tip

Paper crafts take on a professional sheen and an elevated elegance. Simply snap that tip onto QuickSwap Housing (which sold separately) and press the "Go!" button on your Cricut Maker to produce crisp, accurate debossed designs. Unlike embossing directories, limiting you to a specific project, this rolling debossing ball, which your Cricut Maker controlled, allows you to customize, personalize, and design with incredible detail. Make a three-dimensional wedding invitation, a monogrammed thank you card, or flourish to gift items, tags, and other products. On foil cardstock, shimmer, coated paper and glitter paper, foil cardboard, and much more, it creates a beautiful effect.

Engraving Tip

Cricut Engraving Tip can leave an indelible mark. Simply snap this tip onto QuickSwap Housing and press the "Go!" button on your Cricut Maker to get professional-looking results. As you write personalized text or make monograms, add decorative flourishes & embellishments, or engrave your best quotes on a keepsake, you'll be amazed. You are using Cricut Aluminum Sheet or anodized aluminum engraved to expose the silver underneath for a striking effect.

Many of you have asked why these new tools aren't compatible with the Cricut Explore machine family. The gold gear-like installation can be seen on the top of the Cricut Maker-designed equipment. That's what connects directly to the Cricut Maker's Adaptive Tool System, allowing it to use the various regulated movements we mentioned earlier. Since the housing technology is different, the tools aren't compatible with Cricut Explore Air family machines.

Chapter 7. Mats

Understanding which cutting mat is best for the project you're working on is vital for using a Cricut machine.

You'll get used to each of the mats until you start using a Cricut. But first, let me tell you a little more about Cricut cutting pads.

The cutting mats are just the same when you're using a Cricut Explore Air or a Cricut Maker. Both tools can also be used for the same components.

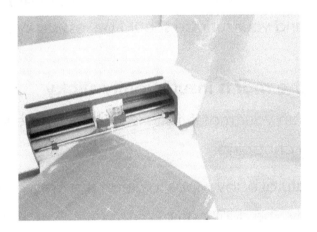

Each Cricut mat was designed to work for a variety of materials and purposes. As a result, each mat has a different grip level.

For heavy designs, others were produced with a solid

adhesive, and some were made with such a soft adhesive to keep the project from ripping or tearing.

Here are few helpful hints for using the Cricut cutting pads and a breakdown of each sheet.

7.1 When your mat is TOO sticky

It may be possible that your cutting mat would be so messy when you first use it, causing you to shred paper or snag materials.

Just use your mat and put the sticky side against your t-shirt or trousers, and your surface should be less sticky now!

7.2 When the mat is insufficiently sticky

You can clean your mat if it sticks to it and materials move about when chopping.

Use some natural baby wipes to clean the area in a circular motion gently. The gunk can begin to fall down. Until reusing the pad, allow it to dry.

A piece of advice: To "restick" the mat, several people recommend spraying it with a sticky adhesive.

7.3 Keep Your Mats Covered

A transparent plastic sheet is included with each cutting pad. PRESERVE IT!!

Try putting the sheet on the mat after each use. It would keep your mat safe and prevent something from sticking to it when you store it.

7.4 Tape Heavy Materials Down

As said earlier that heavy materials like wood and leather should be taped down.

It simply prevents the proposal from progressing into the cutting phase. Notably, if your mat is no longer as sticky, you should do something with painter's tape or washi tape.

7.5 Properly Remove Mat

Often peel your mat away to your project to ensure your design looks awesome, and your mat remains clean.

Carefully peel the mat away from your project by placing it face down on a flat surface.

This would help in the flattening of your project and remove additional materials from your mat, preventing it from being sticky.

7.6 Calibrate Blade for Nice Cut

Make sure that you have the right blade for the job and that the computer is calibrated for it before starting any project.

It greatly aids in ensuring the shortest and cleanest cut possible.

Guide for Cricut Mats

7.7 LightGrip Mat Blue

The LightGrip pad has a light glue grip and is ideal for cutting or removing lightweight fabrics that you don't like to tear or rip.

- Construction Paper

- Lightweight cardstock

- Copy Paper

- Wrapping Paper

- Vellum

- Washi Tape Sheets

- Vinyl

7.8 StandardGrip Mat Green

The basic grip adhesive on the StandardGrip mat will keep on most items you'd use on your Cricut. In crafting, normally, people use the green mat.

- Textured paper or Embossed cardstock

- Cardstock

- Vinyl

- Iron-on Vinyl

- Patterned paper

7.9 Heavygrip Mat Purple

The HeavyGrip mat has a good adhesive that will keep the material in position when cutting.

Taping down the products, such as woods and leathers, is often advised to ensure that they would not slip during the cutting phase. You can do this with painters tape or washi tape.

- Chipboard
- Balsa Wood or Basswood

- Corrugated Cardboard

- Magnet material

- Glitter cardstock

- Fabric with stiffener

- Thick cardstock

- Leather or Faux Leather

- Poster board

7.10 FabricGrip Mat Pink

The FabricGrip pad was created with fabrics in mind. Unlike other cutting pads, this one has a unique adhesive.

One point to keep in mind with this glue is that once it becomes sticky, it won't last as well. Try to keep your palms away from the sticky portion of the mat.

- Crepe Paper

- Bonded Fabrics

- Felt

- Fabrics

7.11 What Size Of Cricut Mat To Use?

Cricut cutting mats are available in two sizes: 12x12 and 12x24.

You'll use the 12x12 pad the most. It's simpler to deal with and suitable for most small tasks.

If you want to sew at all, the 12 x 24 mat is a must-have.

You'll like to be willing to cut out several quilt blocks or bigger template and fabric sections at once. It would be possible for the 12 x 24.

Chapter 8. Storage

With a vinyl cutting machine, you can create an infinite number of crafts and pieces. If you have some crafting bloggers that you follow? There's a good chance they've got some free SVG files & Cricut tutorials! What's even more impressive is how much materials you'll collect when you start making your own.

8.1 Cricut Storage: Be Practical

It would be best if you were realistic when it comes to arranging the cutting machines and materials. Keep the organizational processes clear, and you'll be more able to keep them up to date.

Don't save more than you'll like. That piece of advice is appropriate for every space in your home!

These ideas can help you manage your Cricut storage issues if you're a beginner crafter or an expert at vinyl cutting ventures. These suggestions come from other professional crafters who understand what it's like to arrange vinyl cutting materials.

8.2 Cricut Storage Cart

The first concept is ideal for crafting in confined spaces. To keep it apart and balanced, use a multi-level trolley with wheels.

IKEA has some excellent rolling carts that are ideal for storing vinyl and paper. Hey, let's make things repurposed IKEA Alex Drawers to create the perfect way to organize six different vinyl styles.

A cart with wheels has the advantage of being able to be stored in a corner and brought out as needed without the need for heavy lifting.

Make sure your storage cart has loads of drawers or tiers, regardless of where you purchase it. You'll get a better bang for your buck this way.

8.3 Hang Vinyl On The Wall Rack

With a wall organizer from ArtBin, you can hang vinyl on the wall. The best part about this organizer is how simple it is to assemble. It just clips together and can then be hung on your wall. Your whole vinyl collection is within control.

For holding vinyl, Sweet Red Poppy has devised a brilliant IKEA hack. She took garbage bag holders, hung them on her wall, and then filled them with vinyl rolls. It's crazy how many rolls they can hold and how easily they can be accessed.

8.4 Cricut Storage Cabinet

If you're passionate about your vinyl crafts, you'll want to invest in a perfect cabinet. Whatever kind of cutting machine you have, a storage cabinet like this will make all the changes in life!

It is referred to as the WorkBox because it is a significant expenditure. It is pretty much a crafter's fantasy come true. It includes all of the required totes, drawers, and shelves. The table is foldable. When you're done, you should shut it again. It is **speechless**!

8.5 Labeled Buckets

Many people save money by keeping all of their supplies organized on a bookshelf. Baskets don't have to be expensive; simply purchase some cheap buckets & baskets and name them.

If you have more items to store than fit in stackable containers, the buckets are a better option. They make good use of the available room and keep it enclosed.

8.6 Cricut Storage Bag

If you want to shield your computer from dust or cart it around, you'll need a Cricut storage pack. Choose a backpack that is insulated and has shorter pockets for different tools. This one has it all, and it folds up small enough to go in your luggage.

8.7 Cricut Cartridge Storage

Cricut cartridges might be a thing of past, but certain people still use them. You used to use cartridges with designs on them before the internet and the freedom to bind your Cricut to your device.

If you have a Circut machine and still choose to use the cartridges, organize them in a bin or a storage binder.

8.8 Cardstock Paper Organizer

Holding and color and print apart is the perfect way to hold all of the scrapbook paper & cardstock organized.

Build a wire paper display shelf if you're serious about card production. It is beautiful, much like the way paper is displayed in art stores.

Another choice is to keep the cardstock in work ticket holders made of plastic. Then it would be best if you put them on a shelf or in a file cabinet vertically. It shields the documents from dust and moisture.

8.9 Store Your Supplies On A Peg Board

With pegboard walls, one can store a lot of items in an ordered manner.

In the sewing space, Hey Let's Make Stuff has a lovely pegboard wall. Take a look at the rest of the craft space – it's jam-packed with inspiring ideas!

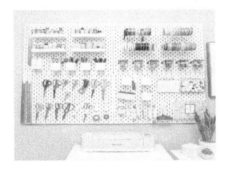

8.10 DIY Cricut Tool Organizer

There is a variety of cutting machine organizers available to hold all of the small blades and accessories that your devices need. Stephanie of Crafting in the Rain made her own version. Making your own organizers has the advantage of allowing you to create as many or as few small spaces as you require.

Chapter 9. The Design Space Application

You're trying to figure out how to use Cricut Design Space but don't know where to begin?

Learning a new activity or talent may be daunting at first. We don't know where to begin because there is so much knowledge available, and it's amazing.

This software is the perfect place for us to practice and master it right away.

You see, if you understand what each icon and panel is about, you can dive in and start exploring more and further.

We have a desire to jump from project after project. Hey, that's fine as well. BTDT-However, we agree that learning your job area can assist you in taking your talent to a different stage.

This chapter aims to educate you about each Cricut Design Space Panel and Canvas Area Icon and show you how to use them.

Let's learn together.

Before we get started, let's define the Canvas Region of

Until your designs are removed, the magic happens in the Cricut Design Space Canvas Region.

Design Space is the place where you can refine and arrange your creations. Not only can you use and upload your own images and fonts in this region, but you can also utilize Cricut's premium images & fonts through individual Cricut Access, transactions, and Cartridges.

Let's get started now; we've had the description out of the way.

If you don't understand how to use the Design Space Software, buying a Cricut is a waste of money because you'll need it to cut every project.

In our view, Cricut Design Space is just an excellent medium for beginners, and even if you have zero experience with other design programs such as Photoshop or Illustrator, you may find it to be very easy, despite its intimidating appearance.

If you have experience, you may also use some of Adobe Creative Cloud software or Inkscape. You'll see that this app is a breeze to use. Shapes and Fonts in Design Space are specifically for refreshing the ventures and making minimal designs.

When you log into the Cricut Design Space account, choose to start or update a new project, you'll see a

CANVASS window.

The Canvas Area in the Cricut Design Space software is where you make all of your edits until your designs are cut.

There are so many keys, options, and stuff to do that you can get overwhelmed. Don't worry; we'll be there to cheer you on and encourage you to keep riding.

In this passage below, you'll discover what each and every icon in the Canvas region means. To keep it organized and simple to grasp, we'll divide the canvas into four key areas and four colors:

Top Panel Yellow-Area of Editing

Right Panel Purple-Panel Layers

Canvas Green area

Blue Left Panel - Insert Area

The top panel in the Canvas area is for editing and arranging objects on the canvas. This panel allows you to choose the type of font you want to use and adjust align styles, sizes, and other options.

This panel is divided into two sub-panels. The first one helps you to save, tag, and cut your projects. The second one allows you to edit and monitor the canvas area.

9.1 The Home Page

The home page is the first page which you see when you open the design space. You see the header, projects, banner, and featured material are the four parts of the home page.

There are four Parts In The Home Page

1. Header

2. Banner

3. My Projects, and

4. Ready To Make Projects

9.2 Header

The hamburger is another name for the menu icon. You can now toggle between the home screen and the canvas.

In addition to new machine setup, account details, link cartridges, calibration, Cricut access, settings, and support, this menu includes new machine setup, account details, calibration, link cartridges, Cricut access, settings,

& help. You may change the units displayed in the settings tab or switch off the grids on the canvas.

9.3 Banner

The carousel in this segment scrolls through a selection of the featured slides. This is where you'll find new information, special deals, maintenance notices, and new items.

9.4 My Projects

Your projects are listed here, sorted by the date they were last opened. To see them together, choose Display ALL. It is the place where you can look for a particular project by scrolling through the list.

9.5 Ready To Make Projects

The following banners show projects that are ready to make and are organized by category. Projects from Cricut Access projects based on materials and projects based on machines will all be featured here.

9.6 The Canvas

You can access the canvas from three separate areas on the homepage, as seen here:

In the Canvas section, there are three toolbars. The header, the design panel, and the layers toolbar are all visible. They are labeled as follows:

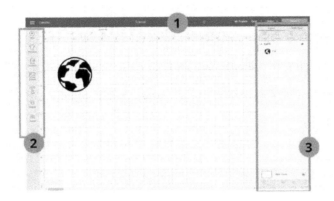

The Header

The menu, project names, machine selection menu, and green Make It button are all found in the header.

Select through the machine you will use to ensure that the appropriate menus and tool options are available.

Design Panel

New

This will bring up a new canvas page with a blank canvas.

Templates

Templates serve as a guide to size and scale. This picture will not cut; instead, it will show on the canvas how big your shirt or the personalized item is so you can scale your design appropriately.

Projects

Look for pre-made prototypes and project ideas. Projects may be classified into a variety of categories, such as project type, season, or case. Featured crafts, Cricut entry, cards, infusible ink, iron-on, sewing, knife blade, and planners are just a few examples.

Images

Browse, pick, and insert images to the Canvas from Cricut Image Library, as well as your own uploaded images.

Text

Fill the Canvas with terms and phrases. The Text Edit toolbar should appear once the text has been inserted. Take a look at the Top Cricut Fonts.

Shapes

Add simple shapes to the Canvas, such as circles, triangles, squares, and lines. You can do a lot of stuff with

simple shapes to build and customize your projects. In a
later guide, we'll go over this in greater depth.

Upload

Cut your own photos for free by uploading gif., png., jpg.,
bmp.,dxf., or svg picture files. For more information about
how to upload your picture, check out this guide.

Layers Panel

Each object in your designs will be displayed on its own layer in the layers panel. Each layer's color selection is critical because it will group all the same color layers on the same cutting mat.

Any pattern that appears as teal on the same piece of paper has been cut out. You can switch the pieces individually and then change the line form using the layers (if it will cut, draw, emboss, etc.). If you're making a card with a shape cut out and a score line, score line the card and cut should all be on the same layer and adhered together.

Chapter 10. Creating An Official Cricut Account

To use Cricut machines, you must first sign up for a free Cricut account. Cricut's software program, Design Space, is used to develop and design files that your machine can understand.

10.1 How To Create An Account at Cricut's Website

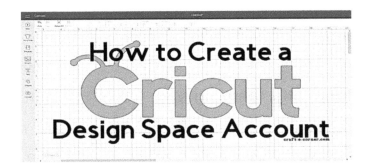

You can access your saved templates, tasks, payment information, and related cartridges by creating an account. It's also fairly simple; let me walk you through the process.

You can build a Cricut DesignSpace account for free by going to design.cricut.com, if you just got the new Cricut machine, are thinking about having one, or just want to create or edit designs in DesignSpace.

Welcome to the Cricut family
Let's set up your machine, create a Cricut ID, and make a fun project!

The first thing you'll need to do is create a Cricut ID., Chose your country (United States, UK, or Canada) from the drop-down window after entering your first & last name and email address. Select the United States or the nearest alternative to your true location when you're not in one of the above three nations. Read and understand the Cricut terms of service, then check the box showing that you understand and approve them: Consider checking the box at the bottom to "Send me Cricut Tutorials, Deals and Inspiration via email" before submitting the details. Cricut will send you an email with sales, inspiration, new releases and other information around once a week. You should uncheck the box that says "never" if you don't want to get these types of emails. Leave the option checked if you'd like to give it a shot. You can unsubscribe at the end of the email or edit your settings in your account if you make your decision later.

Create a Cricut ID

Your Cricut ID is your sign-in for everything you do with Cricut.
Important: Please make sure you create the account as the owner of the new machine.

First Name   Email / Cricut ID

Last Name   Retype Email / Cricut ID

Country   Password
    Please Select   ⌄

◯ I accept the Cricut Terms of Use
☑ Send me Cricut tutorials, inspiration, and deals via email

Already have a Cricut ID?
[Sign In]

After you've done that, press Create User ID. After receiving confirmation of your new account establishment, click Next:

Account created

Your Cricut ID can be used to sign into Design Space, Cricut.com or any other Cricut application.

You have successfully created a Cricut ID!
[Continue]

Cricut asks you a few questions on the next screen to get to recognize you better:

Getting to know you

Where did you FIRST hear about this Cricut machine?	Please Select
Have you owned another Cricut machine?	Please Select
How would you describe your experience level as a DIY crafter?	Please Select

These are only questions to help Cricut figure out who their target audience is. Choose the most reliable option from the drop-down menu.

Install the plugin for Cricut Design Space. It is free software you'll use to create designs with your Cricut machine. Select Download from the drop-down menu.

Get Cricut Design Space plugin

Design Space is your free online software that lets you design, preview, and make projects. It's full of images, inspiration, and more!

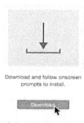

Download and follow onscreen prompts to install.

Download

If you have downloaded the plugin update and are still on this screen, please click here.

A setup wizard will appear and guide you through the entire process. Move on to the next step:

After reading and accepting the terms of service agreement, select the radio button that says "I approve the agreement." To download, you must accept terms and conditions of use. However, it is highly advised you to read them before confirming that you accept them. Select "Install >" from the drop-down menu:

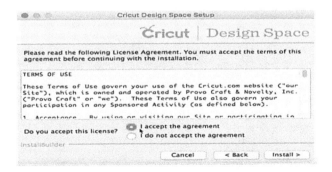

After that, Design Space will begin to install on your computer:

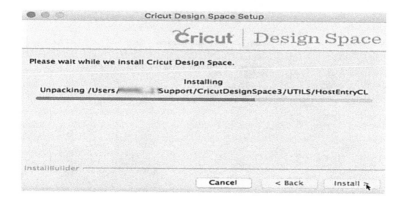

When the plugin will complete installing, and a confirmation screen will appear. Select "Done"

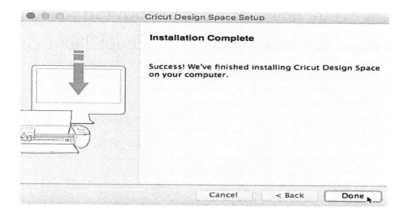

A final confirmation window will appear; click to continue:

Cricut Design Space plugin installed

Successfully installed version 5.5.0.71

Continue

You're now able to start the machine. You can skip this stage if you don't have a machine and just have your account set up. If you have a Cricut machine, turn it on by pressing the power button.

Connect machine

Connect your Cricut machine to your computer with the USB cable and power it on.

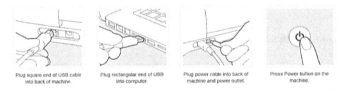

Plug square end of USB cable into back of machine.   Plug rectangular end of USB into computer.   Plug power cable into back of machine and power outlet.   Press Power button on the machine.

Note: Ensure there are 10 inches of space in front and back of machine.

Click the Continue in the bottom of the right corner once you're paired. After that, Cricut will search to see if your machine's firmware requires an update. Continue by pressing the arrow.

The following screens will appear with the text "Get your gifts," which will allow you to enable your free Cricut Access trial subscription for two weeks. You can allow it at a later date if you want to wait until you have more details.

Now that you have:

- Signed up your Cricut ID

- downloaded software

- and updated your firmware

You have the option of beginning to label the sample project or to begin experimenting with the program.

If you ever need to access your Cricut account, go to design.cricut.com and insert your email and password:

Sign In with your Cricut ID

Use your Cricut ID for everything you do with Cricut.

Email/Cricut ID

Password

Please enter your password

Forgot?

☑ Remember Me

Don't have an account yet?

Create A Cricut ID

But if you're using a public or shared screen, make sure the "remember me" box is unchecked. If you choose to Remember Me, your email address will be saved in the Email/Cricut ID folder. If you're using a shared device and don't want your email address to be exposed, uncheck the box. If you're using your device, this box will save you from having to type in your email address every time you log in.

You can log out of your account by going to the main menu then selecting "Sign Out" at the end.

Chapter 11. Design Space On Mobile Devices

Cricut now has an "Online" version that required access to the Internet. You can use the App offline from your desktop or iOS device once you've downloaded it (NOT ANDROID).

No matter what gadget you have, there are three important steps to connecting & setting up your Cricut.

1. Installing Design Space App

2. Connect the machine with your device

3. Logging into your Cricut account and setting up your machine.

Since each operative system is unique, the first two steps appear differently on each device. However, since you'll be using the same interface, pairing your device with your Cricut Accounts would be very similar.

11.1 Install Design Space, Pair Cricut Machine to ipad/iPhone

Before you begin, make sure that your Cricut Machine is turned on and you are 10 to 15 feet far from your iPhone/iPad.

Note: To use your Cricut Explore One with your phone, you'll need a Bluetooth adapter.

Install Design Space software on iPhone/iPad

In order to get Design Space for your iOS device, go to the "App Store" and check for "Cricut Design Space" in the search box.

When it appears in the search results, tap the small cloud icon to save it to your tablet.

When the update is over, tap open to start using the App.

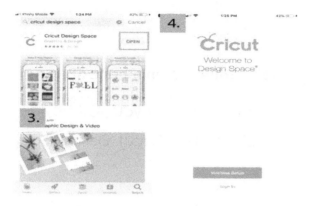

You must first pair your Cricut to the iPhone/iPad before proceeding with the "Machine Setup."

11.2 Connect Cricut Machine to iPhone/iPad

Select "Bluetooth" from the "Settings" menu to pair your Cricut device.

If your Bluetooth setting is off, turn it on so your phone can search for your device.

Remember to turn on your Cricut machine.

Your device will appear under "My Devices," and you can attach it to your phone by tapping on it.

When prompted for a PIN, enter 0000. (no matter which machine you have).

Return to the App to configure your machine.

11.3 Install Design Space, Pair Cricut to Android Tablet/Phone

Make sure your Cricut device is at least 10 feet far from your Android device before beginning the operation.

Note: To use your Cricut Explore One with your phone, you'll need a Bluetooth adapter.

Install Design Space software on Android Devices

In order to get Design Space software on your Android device, go to the "Play Store" and check for "Cricut Design Space" in the search box.

Tap "Install" once it appears in the search results.

When the downloading is over, tap open to begin using the App.

You must first pair your Cricut machine to your phone before proceeding with the "Machine Setup."

11.4 Connect Cricut to Your Android Device

Select "System Link" from the "Settings" menu to pair your Cricut.

Make sure your phone is set to "Enable Bluetooth" so it can find your Cricut machine.

Remember to turn on your Cricut machine.

Under "Available Devices," your computer will appear; tap on it to attach it to your phone. If a PIN is needed, enter 0000 (no matter which machine you're using) and press Connect.

Return to the App to configure your computer.

11.5 Setting Up Your Machine to A Cricut Account

After you've installed Design Space and paired it with your device, you'll need to log in before you can use it.

No matter what machine you have, as you'll see below, the process is nearly identical.

If you're a complete beginner, we suggest starting with "Machine Setup."

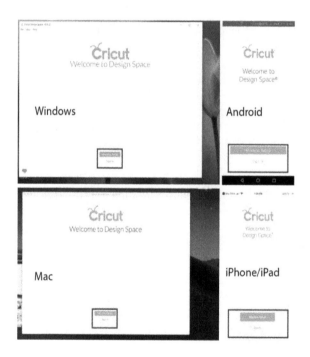

You'll be asked to choose the device you want to pair on the Cricut Setup screenshot. You should have linked your machine to the PC, Mac, or phone via USB or Bluetooth at this stage. Notice that the EasyPress 2 option is not available on iOS or Android devices.

Welcome to Cricut Setup
Select the product you want to set up, register, or update.

Cricut EasyPress® 2

Cricut Joy®

Cricut Maker®

Cricut Explore® family

Fill out the form to build a Cricut ID. If you don't already have an account, click "Sign Up."

This ID can be used to log in to the desktop or mobile App and shop for new machines & materials on Cricut.com.

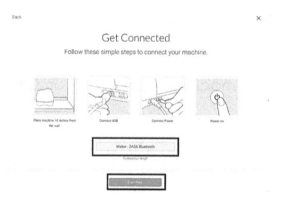

Create a Cricut ID
Your Cricut ID is your golden ticket to all things Cricut.

First Name

Last Name

Country

Please select

☐ I accept the Cricut Terms of Use
☑ Send me free inspiration & exclusive offers.

Email / Cricut ID

Retype Email / Cricut ID

Password

Already have a Cricut ID?

Sign In

Cricut will instruct you on how to attach your machine in the "Get Connected" window (we did this procedure).

Your machine should be linked.

Back

×

Get Connected
Follow these simple steps to connect your machine.

Place machine 10 inches from the wall

Connect USB

Connect Power

Power on

Maker : 2A3A Bluetooth

Connection Help?

Continue by pressing the enter key.

You can now test a cut. It is something advise you to do. Cricut will ask you to select a picture and will guide you through the steps necessary to complete your first cut.

Then press the "Skip" button.

This is the interface you'll see if you're using a Mac or Windows PC.

If you buy another Cricut in the future, launch a "New Machine Set-Up" by clicking the little toggle in the upper-

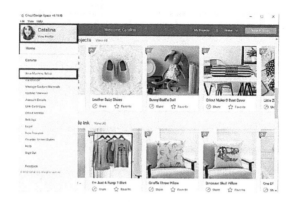

left corner.

This is the interface you'll see if you're operating on your tablet. If you buy another Cricut machine in the future, start again with "New Machine Set-Up" by tapping on the upper-left corner photo.

Wasn't that simple?

You can now begin crafting until your heart's content.

Chapter 12. Design Spaces Canvas

Your projects will be designed on Canvas. You can add & edit projects, images, and text on the Canvas.

Until your designs are removed, the magic happens in the Design Space Canvas Region.

Design Space is the place where you can refine and arrange your creations. Not only can you use and upload your own images and fonts in this region, but you can also utilize Cricut's premium images & fonts through individual Cricut Access, transactions, and Cartridges.

Let's get started now the we've had the description out of the way.

If you don't understand how to use Design Room, buying a

Cricut is a waste of money because you'll need it to cut every project.

In our view, Cricut Design Space is just an excellent medium for beginners, and even if you have zero experience with other design programs such as Photoshop or Illustrator, you may find it to be very easy, despite its intimidating appearance.

If you have the experience, you may also use some of Adobe Creative Cloud software or Inkscape. You'll see that this app is a breeze to use. Shapes and Fonts in Design Space are specifically for refreshing the ventures and making minimal designs.

When you log into the Cricut Design Space account, choose to start or update a new project, you'll see a CANVASS window.

The Canvas Area in the Cricut Design Space software is where you make all of your edits until your designs are cut.

There are so many keys, options, and stuff to do that you can get overwhelmed. Don't worry; we'll be there to cheer you on and encourage you to keep riding.

Here you'll discover what each and every icon in the Canvas region means. To keep it organized and simple to grasp, we'll divided the canvas into four key areas and four colors:

Top Panel Yellow-Area of Editing

Right Panel Purple-Panel Layers

Canvas Green area

Blue Left Panel - Insert Area

Top panel in the Canvas area is for arranging and editing objects on the canvas. This panel allows you to choose the type of font you want to use and adjust align styles, sizes, and other options.

This panel is divided again into two sub-panels. Where the first one helps you to save, tag, and cut your projects. The second one allow you to edit and monitor the canvas.

12.1 Sub-panel #1 Name and Cut your Project

This sub-panel allows to navigate from Canvas area to your projects, profile and also transfers your finished projects to be cut.

Toggle Menu

The entire menu will slides open again if you press this button. Here's a menu that'll come in handy. However, since that's not a part of the canvas, we won't go into great depth here.

You can alter your picture by going to your profile page from here.

You can also do other useful & technical things from this menu, such as calibrating the machine, replacing blades, and upgrading your system's firmware.

In addition, you can manage your Cricut Access accounts, payment details, and more.

We suggest that you click on each connection to learn more about what Cricut Design Space has to offer.

Note: The settings choice allows you to adjust the visibility & measurement of canvas; this is best clarified at the end to go over all about the canvas.

Project Name

After you've put at least one feature, all projects begin with an *Untitled "title" (shape, image, etc., here can only name any project from the canvas).

My Projects

When you tap on my projects, you'll be taken to your library of items you've already created; this is useful because you may want to re-cut a project you've already made. As a result, you won't have to recreate the same project over & over again.

Save

This choice will become active after you've put one element on the canvas area. It is suggested that you save your project on the go. Even if the app is in the cloud, if there is a browser crashes, all of your hard work is lost.

Maker-Explore (Machine)

Depending on what type of machine you got, you'll need to choose between another Cricut Joy, Cricut Explore, or Cricut Maker Machine; this is crucial since the Cricut Maker has only available choices that machine.

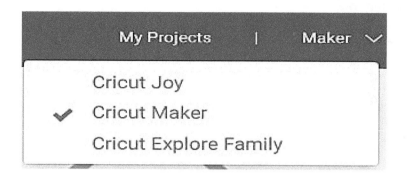

So, if you have got a Maker and design it, you won't be able to use the Maker's software if the Explore feature is turned on.

The different choices for line type are. (We'll be covered here)

Make it

When you're done, click Make it to upload your files, prepared to be cut.

A screenshot of what you'd see is shown below. Mats are used to differentiate the projects based on their colors.

This window also allows you to increase the total of projects to be cut; this is useful if you intend to make several cuts.

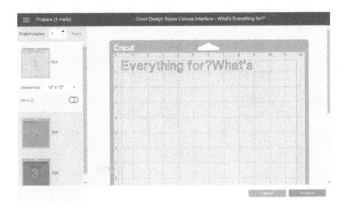

12.2 Subpanel #2 – Editing Menu

Arranging, editing, and organizing fonts and photos in the Canvas Area is extremely useful.

Undo & Redo

We all make mistakes at work from time to time. The use of such tiny buttons is an excellent way to correct them.

When you make a mistake or create something, you don't like, press Undo. Click Redo if you unintentionally delete or modify something you didn't intend to delete or alter.

Fill and Linetype

This choice instructs your machine as to which tools and blades you can use.

Please Keep in mind that it depends upon what machine you choose at the top of window, you'll have different choices (Explore, joy, or Maker).

Line type

This choice instructs your computer which tool to use when cutting your project. Right now, you have eight options (Cut, Draw, Engrave, Deboss, Wave, Score, Perf, and Foil).

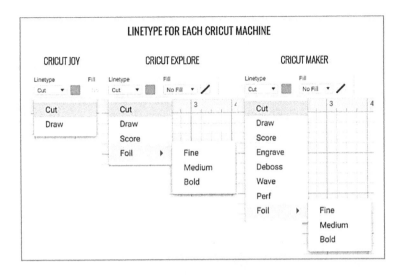

If you got a Cricut Maker, you'll have access to all options; if you do have an Explore, you'll be able to draw, score, cut, and foil; and if you got a Cricut Joy, you'll just have access to Cut & Draw.

Here's a more in-depth overview at each instrument.

Cut

Unless you've uploaded a JPEG and PNG image to a canvas, "Delete" is the default line form for all of your elements; its mean that when you click MAKE IT, your machine will start cutting such designs.

With the Cut choice chosen, you can adjust the fill of elements, which, at the conclusion of the day, translates to the different colors of the materials you'll use to cut your projects.

Draw

If you'd like to write about your projects, you can do that with your Cricut Machine.

When you allocate this line form, you'll be prompted to choose from any of your Cricut Pens (You require specific pens or unless you have the third-party adapter). When you pick a particular template, the layers on the canvas area will be highlighted with the pen color you choose.

When you use this method, the Cricut can write or draw rather than cutting when you press Make it. Notice that this choice will not change the color of your templates.

Score

The left panel's score is a more efficient version of its scoring line. When you allocate this attribute to a single layer, all the designs will show scored or dashed.

When you click Make it this time, you will be taken to a page where you can enter your details. You won't be able to cut with your Cricut, but you will be able to score with your materials.

For these ventures, you'll should have a scoring stylus or just a scoring wheel. Anyway, keep in mind that the wheel is only compatible with the Cricut Maker.

Engrave

It enables you to engrave a variety of materials. Monograms on anodized aluminum or aluminum sheets, for example, may be used to highlight the silver underneath.

Deboss

This tip will help move the material in, allowing for the creation of beautiful and detailed designs. And the debossing tip can allow you to customize your designs at a new level.

Consider making a lovely gift box with roses, stars, hearts, and other decorations.

Wave

Rather than cutting straight lines like a fine point or rotary blade, this method can create wavy patterns on your final cuts.

Curved lines are difficult to achieve in Design Space, and if you're into these impacts, this tool would come in handy.

Perf

The Perf Blade is a tool which allows you to cut materials in small, uniform lines to produce perfect & crisp tear results, such as those seen on raffle tickets, coupons, cards, and tear-out.

Find out how to use a puncture blade.

Foil (New)

Cricut's newest tool is foil, and you can create beautiful foil finishing on your projects by using the Cricut foil exchange kit.

When using this line style, you choose between good, medium, or bold finishes.

Fill

Printing and patterns are the primary uses for the fill option.

Only when you have "line form" Cut will it be enabled. You won't be printing anything if you choose No Fill.

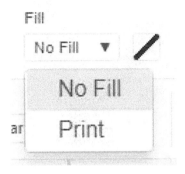

Print

The print feature by far is one of Cricut's great attributes because it enables you to print and then cut your designs; it's fantastic, and it's what drew one to get a Cricut device in the first place.

We made a lot of printable for kids and adults, and we had to cut it for our stories.

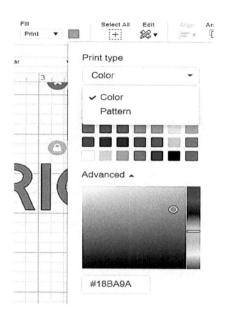

In any case, we're returning to the printing option. As this Fill button is clicked, your files will be sent to your home printer first, and then your Cricut will handle the rest after you press Make it. (Attachment)

Patterns are another excellent print form. This is fantastic. Use Cricut's options or upload your own; also you can apply a pattern to almost any sort of layer.

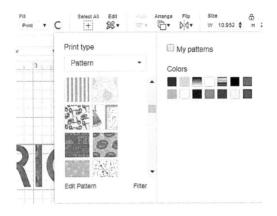

Let's pretend Valentine's Day has arrived. You can make a lovely card using Cricut Access (paid membership), or you can make your own using a pre-made pattern. Then print & cut at the similar time.

The Cricut Maker and some of the Explore Family Devices are only compatible with Fill and Print, then Cut (Cricut Joy is not compatible).

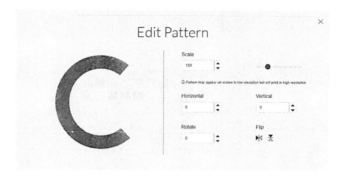

Edit Pattern

Scale
100

Horizontal
0

Vertical
0

Rotate
0

Flip

When you want to transfer all of your elements within the canvas field, you can find it difficult to pick them one by one.

Select All

Tab select all to select all the items on the canvas.

Edit

This symbol allows you to cut (remove from the canvas), clone (replicate an object but retain the original), and

paste objects from the canvas

There is a drop-down menu on the Edit Icon.

When you use a set of one or more elements from the canvas area, the cut and copy option becomes available. When you copy and cut something, the paste feature is allowed.

Align

This menu would be familiar to you whether you've dealt with any design experience that has previews.

If you're new to Align Tools, here's something to keep in mind: the Align Menu is something you'll want to learn.

We'll make a full guide for this, but for now, here's how each align function does.

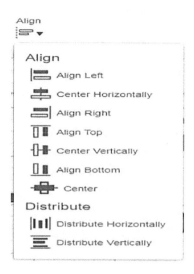

When two or more items are chosen, the Match function is activated, which aligns all of your designs.

Many of the elements will be positioned to the left while you use this setup. Many of the other modules would flow into the component that is furthest to the left.

Center Horizontal: This option will coordinate the components horizontally, with maximum emphasis on text and images.

All of the components would be oriented to the right while you use this setup. All other components can flow through the component that is furthest to the right.

Align Top: This option would make the top fit the rest of the layouts you've chosen. All other components would move through the part furthest away from the tip.

Vertically Centered: This option would vertically align the components. It's easier to work with columns when they're organised and balanced.

Align Bottom: This option aligns your page's bottom with all of the templates you've chosen. The factor that is furthest from the bottom decides where all of the other elements will go.

This is an excellent option for the middle. When you click "align," one configuration is horizontally and vertically balanced to another; this is especially helpful when you choose to centre text for a pattern like a square or a circle.

Distribute: Making it by hand takes a very long time and it's not always correct. You will do this by pressing the Distribute icon. It can only be turned on if you've selected at least three components.

Horizontally Distribute: The objects would be distributed horizontally using this button. The designs on the farthest conservative and liberal would determine the distribution's length, meaning that the items in the centre would be split between the two designs on the widest left and right.

Vertically Distribute: The items would be distributed vertically via this button. The period of the distribution will be determined by the top and bottom models with the greatest distance between them; this ensures that the objects in the centre will be separated between the top and bottom models with the greatest distance between them.

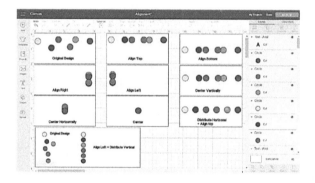

Arrange

The latest creations you put to the canvas were always at the forefront of everything while interacting with many images, text, and crafts. On the other side, all of the layout's elements must be in the and front back.

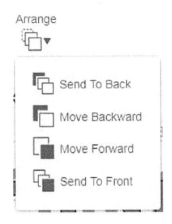

Arrange

Send To Back

Move Backward

Move Forward

Send To Front

Using the arrangement option, you can easily organise the components.

The programme will tell if an item is on the rear or front, but when you select it, Design Space can show you all of the possible options for that feature. Isn't that great?

What are the options available to you:

Return to sender: The chosen element would be pushed to the back.

Step Backward: This option returns the selected object one stage up. That is, if you have a three-element architecture. On a cheese sandwich, it'll feel like honey.

Advancing the Component: This option advances the component by one point. If you do have four or more items to coordinate, you may usually use this option.

This option brings the chosen function to the foreground and leaves it there for the duration of the session.

Toss the coin

This is a good approach to use if you need to represent any of the designs in Cricut Design Space.

There are two possibilities:

Flip Horizontal: It will horizontally replicate the picture or design. It's similar to a mirror in that it comes in useful for doing left and right patterns. If you're making any wings already have the left hand, for example, you can just copy and paste it into Flip and voila. All (left and right) wings are now available to you.

Vertical Flip: This choice flips the designs vertically. It's the same feeling as finding yourself mirrored in glass. This option is perfect if you want to generate a shadow effect.

Dimensions

In Cricut Design Room, anything you create or form has a size. You have the option to adjust the element's size. On

the other side, if you'd like a precise figure for an item, this option would enable you to do so.

Size

W · 5.181 H 1.11

The small lock is extremely important. When you increase or decrease the size of a picture, the proportions are always locked. By clicking upon this small lock, you're telling the software that you don't want to retain the same measurements.

Rotate

Changing the size or rotation of an element can be done easily from the canvas region. In the other side, certain versions may be rotated at a certain inclination. If this is the situation, we recommend that you make use of this function. Otherwise, you'll waste a lot of time trying to get a part to angle correctly.

Rotate

0

Position

Position

X 3.558 ⇕ Y 0.081 ⇕

When you tap on a design, a box appears that tells you where the items are in the canvas area.

You will rearrange the elements by determining where they should be on the canvas regions. It's beneficial, but it's a more sophisticated technique.

We don't even use it too much since the alignment methods we mentioned earlier make getting around much easier.

The typefaces

You can use any font you like for your designs when you

click on this panel. You can philter them and search the top of the screen for them.

If you have Cricut Access, you can get any of the fonts that have a small green A at the beginning of the font description.

If you don't have connections to a Cricut, be sure to use the fonts included with your operating system; else, you'll be fined when your project is cut.

Style

You should adjust the style of your font after you've selected it.

You can choose from the following options:

Regular: That's the default setting, and your font will not alter appearance.

The text will be thickened. Bold: The font would be thickened.

If you prefer italic, the text would be rotated to the right.

Bold italic: In bold italic, the font would be bolded and pointed to the right.

Font size, line spacing, and letter spacing

These choices are fantastic, and we can't recommend them highly enough. The letter spacing, in particular.

You may adjust the font size manually from here. In most cases, it simply alters the text size in the canvas segment.

Letter Space: There is a large difference between each letter in certain fonts. You can conveniently reduce the amount between letters by selecting this choice. Without a question, it's a game-changer.

Line space: This option deals with the space between line in a paragraph; it's handy since we're often required to write a text file due to line spacing issues.

Alignments are essential.

It isn't the same as "orientation" listed previously. For paragraphs, this is the choice.

You have the following options:

Align to the left of a line. Align to the middle of a paragraph.

Align to the right of a paragraph.

Curvature

With this choice, you can be more creative with your email.

You will use this tool to curve the text; the easiest way to learn how to use it is to play around with the little slider.

The text would bend upwards when the slider is moved to the west, and inwards when the slider is moved to the right.

If you move the lever all the way to the left or right, the font can form a circle.

Take Action Now

On the editing panel, Advance is the last choice.

Don't be scared off by the drop-down menu's name. You'll find that after you've heard about all of the solutions, they're not as complicated to use as you would imagine.

Ungroup to Letters: Use this option to cut each letter into a single layer if you plan to alter each character (we'll go through Layers later).

Ungroup to Lines: This option is excellent since it helps you to break up a paragraph into separate parts. Once you've finished typing your paragraph, click Ungroup to Lines to separate into it's own line, that you can now edit.

Ungroup to Layers: Of all the options, this is the most difficult.

This option is only available for Multi-Layer fonts, which can only be bought separately or via Cricut Access.

A multi-layer fonts is one that has more than one layer; these fonts are ideal for adding shadows and colours.

What if you don't like the extra layer of a multi-layer font? To divide each sheet, select the text and then click Ungroup to Layers.

Conclusion

You will want to cut different shapes if you want to create decoration designs and pieces right at home. And although you can do it with a blade, it isn't the most time-saving or simple option. In such instances, one of the excellent Cricut machines mentioned earlier in this section should be considered.

You'll also find a comprehensive purchase guide for these Cricut machines. And, based on all of this information, here are our top list of the best Cricut machines available:

Cricut is an excellent cutting tool that makes it simple to cut the templates you like. It's not only simple and effective, but it's also one of Cricut's best-selling products, and some may even argue that it's the best one available.

This book is an excellent starting point for newcomers to the Cricut culture. You will learn the fundamentals of using the device, and the various device types appropriate for you and set up the Cricut machine. Beginners can learn to use the gripping pads, equipment, and what kind of adjustments should be used to produce the desired outcome in a whole chapter devoted to beginners' crafts. Technical prototypes are often used, in addition to recommendations and feedback. The device may be used for various projects, including home accessories, wedding signs, dolls, handmade cards, party decor, and more.

We hope that this Cricut for Beginners guide can help you learn how to create a basic project and overcome Cricut's unfamiliarity.

Choosing the right Cricut machine for you will make a huge difference in your carving endeavors. With too many options, you need to make sure you choose what you know would perform and help you crafting you want to do.

Do keep in mind that the costliest gadget with all the extra bells and whistles isn't always the right one. To create upscale and one-of-a-kind crafts, you'll want to make sure you're choosing quality.